Illustrated Classics

The Three Musketeers

Please visit our Web site at: www.garethstevens.com
For a free color catalog describing Gareth Stevens Publishing's
list of high-quality books and multimedia programs,
call 1-800-542-2595 (USA) or 1-800-387-3178 (Canada).
Gareth Stevens Publishing's fax: (414) 332-3567.

Library of Congress Cataloging-in-Publication Data available upon request from publisher.
Fax (414) 332-2567 for the attention of the Publishing Records Department.

ISBN-13: 978-0-8368-7664-2 (lib. bdg.)

This North American edition first published in 2007 by
Gareth Stevens Publishing
A Member of the WRC Media Family of Companies
330 West Olive Street, Suite 100
Milwaukee, WI 53212 USA

English translation: Belinda Bjerkvold
Gareth Stevens editor: Gini Holland
Gareth Stevens art direction: Tammy West
Gareth Stevens cover design: Scott M. Krall
Gareth Stevens production: Jessica Yanke and Robert Kraus

Printed in Canada

1 2 3 4 5 6 7 8 9 10 10 09 08 07 06

Illustrated Classics

The Three Musketeers

Alexandre Dumas

GARETH**STEVENS**

GS PUBLISHING

A Member of the WRC Media Family of Companies

On the first Monday of April 1625, fighting broke out in the streets of a small French village. Women fled with their children. Men ran from their houses, waving their swords.

Many people of the village raced to the edge of town, where a small fight had exploded. The fight started when a stranger — dressed all in black and wearing a black patch over one eye — made fun of a young man from the village. The young man drew his sword. The townspeople rushed toward the man in black, but when he pulled out his sword, the townspeople ran away in fear.

The man in black had the young man alone. The stranger threatened the young man with his sword, stole a letter from him, jumped back on his horse, and galloped away. But the struggle was not over. These two would meet again. They had started a rivalry that would last a long time.

It was a time of many power struggles in France. French King Louis XIII struggled against the powerful church leader Cardinal Richelieu. Others, including the English, made war against the King. Queen Anna, the King's wife, hated Cardinal Richelieu. She was also afraid of her husband. In the streets of France, thieves and beggars were everywhere, fighting like wolves against everyone.

The young man was only eighteen. He had dark hair and the long jaw that was common in a person from Gascony, a province on the southwestern coast of France. His eyes were intelligent. His nose hooked like a hanger. He wore a flat, round cap with a feather in it, and he rode a small, strong horse. Anyone would think he was a peasant, except for the sword that hung at his waist. The young man's name was d'Artagnan.

D'Artagnan had left Gascony with the dream of becoming a musketeer. Musketeers protected the King. He carried the gift of his father's sword, the sword of a musketeer. His greatest treasure, however, — the treasure that made him strong — was the advice his father gave him as he was leaving:

"My son, when you get to the King's court, remember that you are a gentleman. The men of our family have been proud gentlemen for the last five hundred years. Do not trust anyone who is not with the King or Monsieur de Tréville, the leader of the King's guard. I give you this letter to Monsieur de Tréville. Hand it to him, and he will make you a musketeer, as I once was."

His father went on, saying, "Travel with courage, not with tricks. You have two reasons to be brave. The first is that you are from Gascony. The second is that you are my son. Look for adventures. I have taught you to fight. You have legs of iron and fists of steel. Fight for the King when you have the chance. I can give you only fifteen coins, this horse, this letter, and the words you have just heard."

D'Artagnan was on his way to Paris, the capital of France, to ask Monsieur de Tréville to make him a musketeer, when the man in black stole his father's letter! D'Artagnan decided he would introduce himself to Monsieur de Tréville without the letter. As he rode into Paris, his horse seemed too small for a real musketeer so he sold the horse for three coins and walked into the city, carrying only a small bundle of belongings.

It did not cost d'Artagnan much to rent a cold, attic room. He put away his things, then left to explore Paris. Close to the river, he came upon a musketeer.

"Where is the house of Monsieur de Tréville, the leader of the King's guard?" d'Artagnan asked the musketeer.

The musketeer pointed to where Monsieur de Tréville lived. Luckily, it was close to the room d'Artagnan was renting. This was a good sign! The trip would be a success, thought d'Artagnan. He would become a musketeer in Paris. It was late in the day, so he returned to his room, but he faced his future with hope. He got into bed and fell asleep, dreaming of becoming a brave defender of the King.

As soon as he woke up, d'Artagnan made plans to go to the house of Monsieur de Tréville. His father had said that Monsieur de Tréville was the third most important person in France. The other two were Cardinal Richelieu and the King himself.

The courtyard of the house of Tréville looked like an army barracks, with fifty or sixty musketeers walking around. Upstairs, in a front room of the house, Monsieur de Tréville received visitors, listened to complaints, and gave orders. Tréville had also come to Paris from Gascony, years ago. He had arrived without a penny. He had nothing but his sword. His only riches were his boldness and his brains. Bravery and intelligence had raised him to the highest level. He was now the leader of the guard of King Louis XIII.

D'Artagnan was impressed with the house of Tréville. He had never seen anything like it, but, because he was the son of a musketeer, he was not afraid. As he crossed the courtyard, with his hand on his sword, the eyes of all the musketeers watched him. For a moment, d'Artagnan wondered if he was as brave as he had thought. He felt small among all these strong fighters.

While waiting to see Tréville, he met Porthos and Aramis. From what they said, they were brave and very loyal to the King. These two and another friend of theirs were three musketeers who would soon become his good friends.

"**A**thos! Porthos! Aramis!" Monsieur de Tréville yelled crossly.

Porthos and Aramis marched upstairs to the front room. Athos did not appear. The two musketeers stood silent and as stiff as sticks before their leader. D'Artagnan, who had followed them up the stairs, watched silently.

"Do you know what the King told me yesterday afternoon? Do you know what it was, gentlemen?" Monsieur de Tréville questioned them. The musketeers stared straight ahead.

Angrily, Monsieur de Tréville said, "He told me that, from now on, he, the King of France, will get his musketeers from the Cardinal's guards!"

This insult was well deserved. Six of the Cardinal's musketeers had beaten six of Tréville's in a fight. Athos, their captain, had been hurt.

The two musketeers said " Sorry, Sir!" They did not dare look their commander in the eye.

"You are dismissed!" Monsieur Tréville ordered.

The two musketeers left.

Then, Monsieur de Tréville greeted d'Artagnan.

"In honor of your father, my old friend," said Tréville, "I want to do something for you.

I will help you become a great musketeer."

After that, d'Artagnan began his training. He quickly became best friends with the three musketeers, Athos, Porthos, and Aramis.

13

Cardinal Richelieu wore the red cap and clothing of a high-ranking church official. He had power in the church, but he wanted power in the world as well. One way to get it was to weaken the power of King Louis XIII.

The Cardinal knew that the Queen of France had secretly given her friend, England's Duke of Buckingham, her diamond necklace. Thinking that he could make the Queen look unfaithful to the King, the Cardinal asked the King to hold a royal ball, where the Queen could show off her diamond necklace. Louis XIII spoke with his wife.

"We will soon hold a ball in the palace. I want you to come to the ball, and I want you to wear your best clothes. I also want you to be shining with the diamond necklace I gave you on your birthday."

"Yes," the Queen answered. What else could she say?

"I do not yet know the night of the ball," said the King. "I will ask the Cardinal."

The Queen was worried. "Did the Cardinal ask that I come to the ball?" she wondered as she ran to her rooms. "Is he the one who talked about the diamonds?"

I am lost!" she cried. "The Cardinal knows everything. The Duke of Buckingham has my diamonds, and he is far away in London! What am I going to do? The King will think I am not loyal to him."

"**H**ow can I serve your Majesty?" asked a calm, soothing voice.

The Queen turned around quickly. Madame Bonacieux, who had been straightening the Queen's rooms, stood in the doorway.

"Don't be afraid," said Madame Bonacieux. "I am a good friend of your Majesty."

"How do I know you are not the person who told Cardinal Richelieu that I gave my diamonds to the Duke?" asked the Queen.

"I speak to you from my heart," Madame Bonacieux replied. "Your Majesty is worried about the diamonds. I will find someone who will go to the Duke of Buckingham and bring the diamonds back to you."

The Queen went to a chest and took out a ring that her brother, the King of Spain, had given her. She held out the ring to Madame Bonacieux.

"The money you will get for this ring should pay for the trip to get the diamonds back," she said. The Queen also wrote a letter to the Duke.

Madame Bonacieux took the ring and the letter and hurried to her home. She lived at the inn, below the room where d'Artagnan was staying. When she got to the inn, she heard her husband inside. He was talking with a stranger. She heard the stranger call her husband "friend." Then she heard him offer her husband a bag of money. The money, she knew, was a bribe! Who was this stranger? Was it Rochefort, the captain of Cardinal Richelieu's guard?

Madame Bonacieux wondered if she could trust her husband now, but she decided she would ask him for the favor she needed.

"I must tell you something of great importance," she said to him. "It is something very urgent. You must leave for London."

"So far away?" he complained. "You can't mean it."

"A very important person is sending you," she insisted. "The pay will be great."

"More secret plots?" asked her husband. "I don't understand. The Cardinal . . . "

"Have you seen the Cardinal?" asked Madame Bonacieux.

"His captain shook hands with me today and called me friend. No one has more power than Rochefort to act on the Cardinal's behalf."

Madame Bonacieux knew that the Queen did not trust the Cardinal. She could not tell her husband about the Queen now, but she had promised the Queen she would get the diamonds back. What could she do? Who could she get to go to London and bring back the necklace?

The next day, Madame Bonacieux noticed d'Artagnan. He looked strong, and he wore his sword well. Little did she know that d'Artagnan had been watching her, too. In fact, he had heard her talking to her husband.

When d'Artagnan saw Madame Bonacieux alone, he came to her and said, "I heard you speaking with your husband, madam. You are trapped. I know your husband is working for the Cardinal, and the Cardinal is against the Queen. What the Queen needs is a fearless man who is smart and loyal to go to London. Here I am, at your service."

"How can I trust you?" asked Madame Bonacieux. "You are so young, and you are a stranger in Paris."

"I have friends who can tell you about me," said d'Artagnan. "Will that help you trust me? Do you know Athos, Porthos, or Aramis? They are the King's musketeers. Their captain is Monsieur de Tréville."

"Monsieur de Tréville! I have heard that he is a brave man and loyal to the Queen. But you must promise that you will not betray me to the Cardinal!"

"I will not betray you," d'Artagnan promised.

Sometimes, a person has to gamble everything, thought Madame Bonacieux. She looked at d'Artagnan and decided to trust him.

"Here is the money you will need," she told him. She handed him the ring, the Queen's letter, and the bag of money, stamped with the Cardinal's seal, that Rochefort had given to her husband.

"This bag is from the Cardinal!" exclaimed d'Artagnan. "It will be fun to save the Queen with money from her enemy!"

They started to make plans. Suddenly, they heard voices.

"It is my husband," said Madame Bonacieux. "What will happen if he finds out that his bag of money is gone?"

"Go up to my room," said d'Artagnan. "You will be safe there."

Moving like two silent shadows, they climbed the stairs. D'Artagnan looked through the window and saw that Monsieur Bonacieux was speaking to a man dressed all in black. He wore a black patch over one eye.

"The man in black!" d'Artagnan exclaimed. "He is the same man who insulted me and took my letter of introduction. I swore that I would kill him, and I will."

Monsieur Bonacieux and the man in black did not know they were being watched. They thought Madame Bonacieux was at the palace so they entered the house. D'Artagnan and Madame Bonacieux hid upstairs. They could hear what the men downstairs were saying.

"You made a mistake, not going to London," the man in black said to Monsieur Bonacieux. "You could have had the Queen's letter in your power. The Cardinal would have paid you for that."

"My husband is a traitor to the Queen!" Madame Bonacieux told d'Artagnan.

Shortly after the man in black left, they heard a loud cry. Monsieur Bonacieux had discovered that his bag of money was gone.

23

The trip to England was dangerous. The three musketeers rode with d'Artagnan, but the Cardinal's guards followed them. The guards captured Athos, Parthos, and Aramis, firing muskets at them and waving their swords. Only d'Artagnan was able to reach the port of Calais. He planned to sail from there to England. As d'Artagnan walked toward the port, he saw a man ahead of him, trying to board the ship.

The port guards stopped the man, saying, "We have received an order from the Cardinal not to let anyone board the ship without a letter of permission from him."

"I have the Cardinal's letter," said the man.

"That's good," replied one of the guards, "but the governor of the port will have to sign it."

As the man walked toward the governor's office, d'Artagnan followed him. D'Artagnan knew he must be one of the Cardinal's men. He took out his sword and stabbed the man three times, yelling, "One for Athos, one for Porthos, and another for Aramis!"

As the man lay on the ground, d'Artagnan looked through the man's pockets. He found the Cardinal's letter. He left the man lying on the ground and took the letter to the governor. Thinking that d'Artagnan was one of the Cardinal's men, the governor signed the letter, and d'Artagnan could board the ship.

D'Artagnan's ship had just left Calais when he heard a musket shot. The shot meant that no more ships could leave Calais. The port was closed. D'Artagnan had sailed just in time.

In England, d'Artagnan told the Duke of Buckingham the story of his trip. He told the Duke how the Cardinal's men had attacked the three musketeers. Then he gave the Duke the letter from the Queen.

After reading the letter, the Duke opened the little box where he kept the diamond necklace. The necklace was missing two diamonds!

"Someone has stolen from me!" he cried. "It could only have been Milady, the Countess. She is not to be trusted."

A jeweler worked all night to cut two new diamonds for the necklace. Meanwhile, the London guards stopped all boats leaving for France. This could mean only one thing. France and England were now at war.

D'Artagnan had to get back to France! Luckily, he was able to escape by sailing from a small port on the English coast. He landed at a little town on the coast of France.

D'Artagnan quickly walked to an inn that the Duke of Buckingham had told him to find. The owner gave d'Artagnan a horse for his trip to Paris, and d'Artagnan galloped off. Twelve hours later, he delivered the necklace to Madame Bonacieux. He had arrived just in time!

27

That night, the Queen went to the ball. The diamond necklace sparkled around her neck. The Queen looked happy, and she wore the necklace proudly. As the King and Queen walked in front of Cardinal Richelieu, he felt foolish. All his plans had been ruined.

A few days later, a paid killer attacked the Duke of Buckingham. The Duke was badly hurt. As he lay dying, letter arrived for him.

My Dear Duke,

Do not keep planning a war against France. Cardinal Richelieu is trying to start this war. He wants you to hurt France. Then he will have more power than the King of France! Please help us stop this wicked man. A war would hurt us all.

Yours affectionately,

Queen Anna

The Duke of Buckingham looked at the little box where he had kept the Queen's diamond necklace. It was the only thing he still had from her. Then he took his last breath.

The Duke's brother, Lord de Winter, trapped the Duke's killer very quickly. The killer said he had killed the Duke because he hated him. Lord de Winter did not believe this lie. He was sure that Milady had paid the killer to murder the Duke. The proof was that she had suddenly left for France.

"I swear on the memory of my brother, the Duke of Buckingham, that Milady will not escape!" said the angry Lord de Winter. "She paid this man to kill the Duke!"

Back in Paris, Monsieur de Tréville gave d'Artagnan and the three musketeers six free days. D'Artagnan was in a hurry to meet Madame Bonacieux at the convent of Béthune. She was hiding there to protect herself from the Cardinal. The Cardinal felt she had made a fool of him, and he was very angry.

The three musketeers traveled with d'Artagnan. They wanted to help d'Artagnan protect Madame Bonacieux. Coming to an inn on the journey, d'Artagnan saw the man in black. He was leaving the inn on horseback at full gallop.

"There he is!" yelled d'Artagnan. "I must follow him!"

"Who is it?" the musketeers asked.

"It is the cursed man in black!" said d'Artagnan. Whenever I cross paths with him, something terrible happens."

A servant came forward, holding a paper that had fallen from the man in black. D'Artagnan bought the paper from the servant for a few coins. On it was written the name of a small town — Armentières.

"Forget the man in black," the three musketeers begged d'Artagnan. "Your lady waits for your help."

D'Artagnan and the musketeers galloped off to Béthune. Saving Madame Bonacieux was more important, right now, than fighting the man in black.

Upon arriving in France, Milady wrote to Cardinal Richelieu.

Your Eminence the Cardinal can be happy. The Duke of Buckingham will not come to France. I await your orders in the convent of Béthune.

—Milady

Milady quickly made her way to the convent at Béthune, where the Mother Superior told her that a new woman had arrived who feared the Cardinal. Milady, who served the Cardinal, feared only d'Artagnan and the three musketeers, who were loyal to the King and Queen of France.

Milady asked to meet the new woman. It was Madame Bonacieux. Milady gained Madame's trust and soon found out that d'Artagnan would arrive that night. Hearing the sound of a galloping horse, Milady feared the worst. Milady and Madame watched as the horseman rode up to the convent.

"No, it isn't d'Artagnan," said Madame Bonacieux.

Milady stopped worrying. When the horseman arrived, he asked for Milady. It was the Count de Rochefort, the Cardinal's right-hand man.

33

Milady brought the Count de Rochefort to meet Madame Bonacieux. She lied and said that the Count was her brother. The Count also lied. He told Madame that the Cardinal was sending four men, dressed as musketeers, to kidnap her. The Count said he would send a carriage to help the ladies escape to Armentières. Then he rode off quickly.

Madame trusted Milady. What Milady didn't tell Madame was that the Count de Rochefort was not going to help Madame escape the Cardinal. He would be waiting in Amentières to take Madame to the Cardinal — to be punished!

While they were eating dinner, the women heard horses. It was d'Artagnan and the three musketeers. Milady dropped poison into Madame's glass. Lifting the glass to Madame's lips, Milady said to her, "Drink this. Then let's go quickly, before the Cardinal's men trap us."

Moments after she drank, Madame Bonacieux could not walk. Milady ran to look for her carriage. Falling to the convent floor, Madame Bonacieux heard the voice of her dear friend and called to him.

"Thank God you have come, d'Artagnan. She told me to flee with her."

"She? Who is she?" asked d'Artagnan. "Do you know her name?"

"It was a strange name," Madame whispered. "Milady. . . the Countess . . . oh . . . my head is spinning . . . I can't see anything!"

The poison was taking effect. D'Artagnan held Madame Bonacieux in his arms as her body became stiff and cold. At that moment, Lord de Winter arrived. He was looking for the murderous Milady.

34

D'Artagnan, Athos, Porthos, and Aramis joined Lord de Winter. They tracked Milady's footsteps. So did a strange horseman in a red cloak. Together, they found Milady alone in a country house.

"What do you want?" she screamed. She saw that she was trapped.

"We're looking for Milady, the Countess!" said Athos.

"I am she," the Countess sneered.

"We are going to judge you for your crimes," said Porthos.

"Before God and man," shouted d'Artagnan, "I accuse you of poisoning Madame Bonacieux."

"I accuse you of having assassinated the Duke of Buckingham!" added Lord de Winter. If you are not arrested for these two murders, I will get justice myself."

At that moment, the man in the red cloak, who had been silently watching, uncovered his head.

"The executioner! The executioner!" screamed Milady.

The man in the red cloak broke his silence. "You have murdered others, as well," he said. "You must pay for your crimes. I will take what you owe as soon as a judge decides your sentence."

The executioner tied Milady's wrists and took her as his prisoner. She would kill no more.

The three musketeers rode off, following d'Artagnan at full gallop. Their friendship had been strengthened by success.

"One for all and all for one!" they cried.

Justice had been done.

About the Author

Alexandre Dumas was born in Villers-Cotterêts, in Aisne, France, in 1802. He died in Puys, a French island, in 1870. He wrote 157 novels and 25 plays and is honored today as one of the greatest French novelists of all time. Many movie versions have been made of his works. Among his most famous novels are: *The Three Musketeers*, *Twenty Years After* (which is the continuation of the adventures of the musketeers), and *The Count of Monte Cristo*.